FLORETS OF THE MEADOWS

Poetry Woven In Wildflowers And Wanderings

Dr. Kanchan Birat

BookLeaf Publishing

India | USA | UK

Made with ❤ on the BookLeaf Publishing Platform

www.bookleafpub.in

www.bookleafpub.com

Dedication

To those who seek peace in a world that never stands
still,
To the souls who have achieved much yet still searching
for meaning,
To the dreamers, the wanderers, and the ones who long
to belong-
May you find solace in nature's quiet wisdom and in the
rhythm of these verses.
It is a gentle reminder that we are all part of something
greater.
As a token of Love, last few poems are dedicated to my
family.

-Dr. KB

Preface

Florets of the Meadows is more than just a collection of poems- it is a journey through the heart of nature and the soul of human emotions. Like delicate florets swaying in the breeze, these verses capture the fleeting yet profound moments of life: the serenity of dawn, the dance of the wind through wildflowers, the quiet ache of longing, and the tender joy of love.

Just as spring and autumn shape the landscapes, our lives, too, are shaped by moments of joy and sorrow, growth and stillness, love and longings. We thrive under the sun, endure the storm, and embrace change with the wisdom that is given to us by nature itself. These poems celebrate that cycle, reminding us that even in loss, there is renewal; even in hardship, there is beauty; and even in diversity, there is unity.

Through these verses, I invite you to walk through the meadows of words, to pause and feel the whispers of the wind, to embrace the gentle rhythm of existence. May you find in these pages a reflection of your own journey, a reminder that no matter the season, we continue to grow, to learn, and to bloom.

-Dr. KB

Acknowledgements

Writing *Florets of the Meadows* has been a journey of reflection, growth, and deep gratitude. This book would not have been possible without the love, wisdom, and inspiration I have received from my family. Thank you for being my roots and my wings- for grounding me in love while encouraging me to dream. Your unwavering support has been the foundation of my journey, and I am forever grateful.

To the silent moments in nature, the whispering trees, the blooming flowers, and the dancing winds- you have been my greatest teachers, reminding me of the beauty in stillness, change, and renewal.

And finally, to life itself, with all its seasons- thank you for the lessons, the challenges, and the endless reasons to keep growing, learning, and blooming.

With gratitude

-Dr. KB

1. Susurrations of a Wandering Soul

At times, I yearn to drift afar,
On silver wings where dreamers are.
To touch the blooms, with feet oh! bare,
To breathe their scents blown in the air.

To roam with beasts, untamed and free,
And taste the thrill of liberty.
At times, I long to dive so deep,
Where ocean's mystic secrets sleep.

To waltz with turtles, emerald-bright,
Beneath the waves of fluorescent tide.
To face the giants of the sea,
And feel their power inside me.

At times, I wish to stand so high,
Upon the hills that kiss the sky.
To watch the world in hush below,
To see the restless breezes blow.

To chase the birds, to dance, to glide,
To ride the wind both fierce and mild.
At times, I crave a tranquil stream,
To sit, to drift, to simply dream.

To trace the ripples' fleeting grace,
As water carves its winding space.
To breathe the scent of earth so new,
Where raindrops weave a misty hue.

At times, I seek the fog's embrace,
To watch the golden sun in place.
To see it rise with fiery gleam,
And light the world in golden beams.

To feel its warmth, to see it shine,
To know its strength, so fierce, divine.
At times, I hope for rain's soft song,
To hum where burning hearts belong.

To chase the hues that paint the sky,
And steal a rainbow passing by.
To hold its colors, pure and bright,
And wear them in my soul's delight.

Oh, how I long to see it all—
The seasons rise, the blossoms fall.
The storm, the sun, the skies untamed,
The whispers nature leaves unnamed.

-Dr. KB

2. Nature's Melody

Dawn shines bright on silent hills,
A poet's paintbrush capturing stills.
The wind hums soft, a fleeting rhyme,
Its whispers lost, yet caught in time.

The river sings in silver tones,
Its verses carved through ancient stones.
The trees stand tall, their voices deep,
Their roots hold secrets time will keep.

The flowers bloom in scented prose,
A fleeting song the springtime knows.
The stars blink bright, their hymns unseen,
Yet poets hear where night has been.

The bees when dance, and make the twee,
The nectar falls, breeze bends the tree.
The meadows sway, a gentle grace,
As nature's heart begins to race.

In blade of grass a tale unfolds,
In hues of green, the earth beholds.
The mountains stand like ancient guards,
Their stoic strength in silent shards.

Each shadow fades, as hope ignites,
In every soul, a flame of lights.
So let the pen be swift and free,
In dawn's embrace, our spirits flee.

-Dr. KB

3. Echoes of the Birth

It begins with a cry, entrusting our fate,
To parents whose joy knows no weight.
A mother's gaze, tender yet wise,
Sees the timid dreams in our eyes.

The world foretells, predicts our way,
Molding our future in silent sway.
We tremble, we falter, our minds ensnared,
By voices telling, how to be prepared.

Expectations rise, their shadows loom,
We chase their dreams, despite the gloom.
Lost in echoes, we strive to be,
A reflection of what they wish to see.

Yet, time arrives with a voice so bold,
A whisper of courage, a story retold.
Regrets and mistakes, we carry along,
Yet in the struggle, we find our song.

A glimmer of light, a beacon so bright,
Illuminates truths hidden from sight.
It teaches the soul what it truly needs,
Not hollow applause, but meaningful deeds.

A moment of truth, bitter yet kind,
Reveals the strength we longed to find.
We stake it all, with trust so grand,
Knowing destiny rests in our hand.

With every fall, we rise once more,
Claiming our crown through battles sore.
For life is a tale of lessons untold,
Of suffering, learning, and spirits turned bold.

Each choice we weave, a tapestry spun,
Threads of our past, where battles were won.
In the dance of the now, in the breath of the day,
We learn to embrace what our heart wants to say.

For every tear shed, a lesson is penned,
The journey of self, where beginnings transcend.
And through it all, in joy & lullaby,
It always begins with just a cry.

-Dr. KB

4. Hope- The Eternal Wait

I sit by the shore, still and forlorn,
My heart sways between hope and scorn.

The river glistens, silver and bright,
Yet my eyes glimmer with unsaid fright.

Was it the stream, or a distant cry?
But you had sworn, you will come by.

The sun grew dim, the sky turned gray,
Still, my heart refused to drift away.

The seagulls circle, they dance in despair,
Their cries are mournful, like a lover's prayer.

With weary eyes, I gaze behind,
Tracing the path you left confined.

I call your name, my voices squeak,
The waves respond, but not who I seek.

Here I remain, through time and test,
Hoping you'll return before my rest.

-Dr. KB

5. Silent Blues

High above, you soar so free,
Yet to find a pearl in the sea,
One must dive where shadows gleam,
In depth unknown, where echoes scream.

How long have I stood, waiting still?
How long since your voice went still?
A fleeting glance, a moment bright,
A love once lost in borrowed light.

The angels sang a melody sweet,
Yet I searched places where we meet.
The love I sought was always near,
A murmur soft I failed to hear.

Did you seek me as I did you?
Did you hear the song ring too?
Or was it I who bore the tune,
Lost in shades of silent blues?

Never alone, never in fear,
A promise held forever dear.
Not lost to time, nor dimmed by fate,
Standing strong, I illuminate.

-Dr. KB

6. Resilient Remnants

Standing in the midst of the shore,
I see clearly what's at the core.
No plans, no decisions, no plots to make,
I know it's not a piece of cake.

Only those weary, tattered, and worn,
Can truly connect with those who mourn.
Thrills, shrills, and shouts are there,
Echoes of laughter, sighs of despair.

Do not offer to carry their weight,
Not your baggage, they are your mate,
Do whatever it takes to ignite the fire,
Awaken their courage and inspire.

Be loud, be quiet, embrace the choice,
But never silence your heart's voice.
Regret may bind, remorse may chain,
Yet healing waits beyond the pain.

Repentance, remorse, restrains & more,
May you find what's but the sour,
Restore the pieces, mend them anew,
Reclaim your peace, to shine through.

-Dr. KB

7. Delirium of Awakening

The lavenders, the daisies, the marigold,
No longer mesmerize me as they unfold.
Autumn leaves roar as they descend,
While the restless breeze refuses to mend.

The burning sensation is hard to mold,
My frail body is fiery-cold.
No sound, no words, just quiet despair,
As frost carves shrieks deep in the air.

Crying candles flicker, memories fade,
Brilliance once bright now seems delayed.
Yet under the frost, a promise awaits,
In the silence, a warmth radiates.

The pressure that builds in the head,
Neurons starved, not properly fed.
Emotions falter, movements stall,
A reaching hand, I need, that's all.

A heart weighed down by unseen part,
An art of wounds that won't depart.
For what have we wandered this far,
If we're destined to be a shooting star?

-Dr. KB

8. The Journey

We took a walk, no words to share,
Yet silence spoke, it lingered there.
Two souls adrift, one path to tread,
Unsure of where the journey led.

The sun grew pale, the moon rose high,
The river shone like the silver sky.
Soft ripples danced and sang the song,
As time stood still, yet moved along.

The night was cold, the winds ran free,
But warmth was found, just you and me.
You placed your coat around my frame,
A simple act, but I felt the fame.

Our eyes would meet, then drift apart,
A silent search, a speaking heart.
No need for words, no urge to flee,
Just knowing you were here with me.

A fleeting doubt, a step unsure,
Your hand found mine, a touch so pure.
No end in sight, no place to be,
Just walking on, just you and me.

-Dr. KB

9. The Phoenix Reborn

For all the jovial moments we had,
For all the memories we have shared,
Will surely bless you to the core,
For making me want you many more.

But time has passed, the past has flown,
The weight once heavy, now unknown,
Yet let me paint the tale once more,
Of how your words cut to the core.

No need to dive in wounds so deep,
The scars are mine, they're mine to keep,
You stole my peace & ensured,
My skin, my nail, my height censured

Oh, how you tried to break my light,
To steal my joy, to dim my might,
I foiled your traps & tricks to steal
The joy entrenched & how I feel.

Now I don't care what you believed,
I stand strong here and now relieved,
As I have learned, and now I see,
You hold no power over me.

The mirror, the water, the skies so wide,
Reflect the strength I hold inside,
I never forget to tell the girl,
Embrace the confidence & freely swirl.

No longer bound by what you say,
I've found my worth; I've found my way,
The storm once fierce, now bends, now claims,
I rise like a Phoenix from the flames.

-Dr. KB

10. Eternal Embrace

Drifting down, wrapped in your hold,
Where time stands still, where dreams unfold.
Silence hums in tender grace,
A haven formed in your embrace.

I do not wish to slip away,
Not now, not ever, just let me stay.
For here, the world dissolves to air,
And heartbeats weave a love so rare.

Head resting where your warmth remains,
Half in slumber, no sign of pains.
Of whispered breath and quiet space,
A refuge, time cannot replace.

Barefoot on the murmuring ground,
Where souls entwine yet make no sound.
Between the groove, we coincide,
Hands held fast, fingers tied.

No distant roads, no far-off lands,
No fleeting call, no lost demands.
For here, beneath your soft-lit gaze,
I find my home in endless days.

I do not wish to drift or roam,
Not now, not ever, this is home.
For here is where the blossoms stay,
Where love remains, and won't decay.

-Dr. KB

11. Transcending through the Worlds

It begins where existence unravels,
Souls unshackled, drifting free,
A realm reborn in ethereal glow,
Bound to fate, yet longing to flee.

Crimson blooms and violet flames,
Stars that shimmer, fountains blue,
Mountains forged of crystal light,
A bridge where worlds align anew.

Pristine and untouched, it stands apart,
A sanctuary of white and azure,
Bathed in an ever-present light,
Veiled in mist, serene and pure.

Hand in hand, they tread unknown,
Stripped of burden, hearts laid bare,
No veils to shield, no secrets kept,
Only truth lingers in the air.

Silver rivers whisper softly,
Gardens bloom in emerald hue,
Clouds embrace in endless waltz,
Beneath a twin-lit cosmic view.

Here, the threshold looms between,
The transient and the divine,
Lucifer stands, a silent keeper,
No plea, no lie, no borrowed time.

No words of reason shall suffice,
Only truth may guide you through,
For in this realm of quiet passage,
You are seen for what is true.

Yet shadows dance with twilight grace,
Echoes of a past, a distant sigh,
In the stillness, dreams embrace,
The whispers of an unearthly high.

-Dr. KB

12. Withering reveries

At twilight's hush, I sat alone,
Drifting through the past we'd known.
Fingers curled beneath my chin,
As winds brushed softly on my skin.

The stars awoke in endless night,
Their silver glow so still, so bright.
I thought of you, and there you were,
A memory's touch, a vision quite blur.

I met you once in laughter's glow,
You asked me out, I told you no.
Yet time was kind, it brought us near,
With tender words, you called me dear.

A single rose, a quiet plea,
You knelt and softly asked for me.
I took your hand, our fingers twined,
Believing that love was gentle, kind.

We met beneath the Paris sky,
Where wishes soared and love ran high.
But time can shift, can break, can bend,
What once was whole is now at end.

A decade passed, your heart grew cold,
The warmth we felt, now far too old.
I begged, I wept, yet still you strayed,
And love, once fierce, began to fade.

You seem to think she's falling apart,
But cannot affect or mend my heart.
I'm grateful for my eternal salvation,
No cry, no signs of any palpitation.

I'll weave new dreams with threads of gold,
My wings grew strong, my heart turned bold.
Finally liberated from the pain & lies,
Well, the nectar is truly not for flies.

-Dr. KB

13. Stardust Serenade

I saw you stand, eyes searching wide,
In brown-clad grace, my heart complied.
A fleeting choice, a nervous start,
Yet fate had drawn us, heart to heart.

The sunlit wind, your dark silk hair,
A gaze so deep, I lingered there.
No words were said, yet much was told,
In smiles and blushes, soft yet bold.

The lake reflected whispers true,
Your hand in mine, the world withdrew.
A sleepless night, a dream so bright,
Awaiting dawn, embracing light.

The next day found us side by side,
With bolder hearts, no fears to hide.
Your birthmark's tale, your eyes so deep,
A moment time would choose to keep.

The breeze was cold, yet warmth was near,
A starlit wish, a love sincere.
A tight embrace, a fading sun,
Yet parting's sorrow had begun.

Your laughter lingers through the air,
A symphony of love laid bare.
With heavy steps, I walked away,
Yet in my soul, you'll always stay.

-Dr. KB

14. Celestial Chimera

Let me be the golden dawn,
You, the dewdrop on the lawn.
That I may kiss your tender grace,
And bathe you in my warm embrace.

Let me be the drifting snow,
You, the tree in silent glow.
Softly, I shall weave and twine,
A dance so pure, your limbs entwine.

Let me be the playful rain,
You, the rose in crimson vein.
That I may waltz upon your bloom,
And sprinkle love in sweet perfume.

Let me be the ocean's breeze,
You, the sand where waters tease.
To chase the waves and taste the air,
And leave my touch on you so rare.

Let me be the waterfall,
You, the stone that waits its call.
With every leap, I shall descend,
To meet your soul where rivers bend.

Let me be the breath of spring,
You, the sea, vast & shimmering.
That I may rest upon your shore,
And hold you close forevermore.

-Dr. KB

15. The Unheard Symphony of Her Toil

She rose before the waking sun,
While stars still awake, her day begun.
No time to rest, no dream to keep,
Though weary eyes had pleaded sleep.

She tiptoed past the silent halls,
To heed the cattle's morning calls.
With hands so firm, yet soft with grace,
She lifted the yoke, an endless chase.

An hatchet she wielded, strong and true,
To crack dry wood, the flames she knew.
She donned the logs like hood so light,
Then kindled warmth against the night.

The stove now burned, the tea was poured,
For all but her, the meal was stored.
They ate, they left, no backward glance,
She packed their tins with careful stance.

Her stomach ached, yet none would know,
For sweat must drown the hunger's woe.
She reached the fields, her breath was fleet,
But none would pause, her tale to greet.

Beneath the sun's relentless sting,
She bent and worked, no voice to sing.
The evening came, a fleeting sigh,
Yet duty's chains still bound the sky.

With aching limbs, she cooked once more,
While others dreamed, she scrubbed the floor.
The world lay still in slumber deep,
Yet she toiled on, no time to weep.

For illness, pain, could not be willed,
A woman's work must not be stilled.
For in her travail, a legacy sewn,
A discreet strength, forever known.

-Dr. KB

16. Shadows of The Fallen Age

Vows once spoken, dreams once bright,
Lie abandoned, lost in night.
Revenge and greed now take their place,
Society falls from truth and grace.

Where morals fade and falsehood thrives,
Where justice struggles to survive.
Debates turn hollow, truth lies still,
The deaf obey the lender's will.

Rank and class now blind the eyes,
Binding souls in silent ties.
The weak are trampled, hope is gone,
Liberty stolen, justice withdrawn.

The ones who judge, the ones who lead,
Immortal stand in ruthless greed.
Where demons reign and darkness grows,
The voice of freedom silent goes.

Love and kindness fade away,
As greed now rules the hearts astray.
Weapons forged from selfish needs,
To satisfy the rich man's greed.

The poor now cry, the helpless plead,
Yet none will listen, none will heed.
Innocence lost, the world's grown cold,
Who will rise? Who will hold?

-Dr. KB

17. Whirlwind of Desire

I was a lassie, and you, a bloke,
You spun me 'round like swirling flock.
We twirled like leaves in autumn's flight,
Unsure if it was love or just the night.

You pulled me close, I felt the shift,
A heartbeat's pause, a reckless lift.
Was it a skill or just the thrill?
Your wings had learned, they knew the drill.

I couldn't fight, with feet bare,
Lost in magic, entangled there.
You left a trace, a fleeting spark,
Like fireflies wiggling in the dark.

You moved with ease, Oh! What a grace,
As if you'd been in love's embrace.
I rose in rhythm, in depth of sea,
Locked in waves of ecstasy.

My breath betrayed a stolen glance,
A moment caught in happenstance.
A tangled tune of youth and glee,
Composed in quiet intimacy.

Together lost in a timeless trance,
We found forever in a single glance.
The pulse of love, so wild so free,
A dance we found in you and me.

-Dr. KB

18. Deserted Love

Do not forsake my heart in sand,
Alone, abandoned, lost, unmanned.
I search, I plead, yet find no trace,
Of love once carved in time and space.

You vanished deep into the night,
Leaving me in doubts, a silent plight.
No vows to break, no words to mend,
Just love that obliterated in the end.

I never thought your touch so sweet,
Would leave me drowning in defeat.
I wait for words you never speak,
A love now distant, cold, and weak.

Yet hope remains, it will not die,
Though silence lingers, though you deny.
Come back, my love, don't let me grieve,
I trust in you, I still believe.

Say the words, erase my doubt,
Pull me from this desert's drought.
Love me, hold me, make me see,
You'll bring me back, you'll set me free.

-Dr. KB

19. Sister- A Blessing

Through every season, side by side,
Under one roof, with hearts open wide.

We laughed till dawn, we wiped each tear,
Through every storm, you held me near.

Golden days of childhood bright,
Still linger softly in my sight.

We bickered, we mended, we learned, we grew,
Yet love remained, forever true.

The thoughtful gifts and surprises,
Towers of memory stays our prizes.

Though life has led us separate ways,
Our bond, unshaken, forever stays.

No distance vast, no time unkind,
Can break the love our souls enshrined.

For every hug, for every fight,
For all the ways you made things right.

Thank you, sister, my heart, my home,
With you, I'm never truly alone.

-Dr. KB

20. Mom- The Unwavering

The one who rules the home,
Who sets the rhythm & the norm.

The one whose love is calm yet bright,
Who keeps you safe within her sight.

The one who lulls when we cry at nights,
Who scolds too, when we get into fights.

The one who wakes through weary nights,
Obliviating the fears and silent frights.

The one who teaches with patience profound,
In her warm embrace, peace is found.

With laughter that dances like sun on the sea,
Her heart is the anchor, but the soul is free.

A guide through life's twists, gentle & bold,
Her wisdom, her stories, our memories hold.

A tribute to a woman so strong,
The essence of love, where we belong.

-Dr. KB

21. Dad- The Pillar of Strength

One so calm, yet strong inside,
A sturdy heart, a steady guide.

Who else could hold the sky in place?
A father's love, both strength and grace.

One who shields through storm and tide,
A silent wall where love resides.

Who else could stand through night and day?
A steadfast soul that lights the way.

One who molds with patient hands,
Who lifts us up, yet understands.

Who else could carve the dreams we weave?
A guiding touch we can't deceive.

In laughter shared, in tears we've spilled,

You plant the seeds of hope fulfilled.

Who else could shine with light so true?
A love eternal, deep and through.

This is what the world may see,
A glimpse of all you are to me.

-Dr. KB